Thoroughbred Spirit

SPIRIT OF THE HORSE SERIES

Words By Betsy Sikora Siino

BOWTIE PRESS

Images By Bob Langrish

To my family - always supportive of sprouting wings and chasing after dreams.
—B.S.S.

Ruth Berman, editor-in-chief
Nick Clemente, special consultant
Doug Kraus, designer

The horses in this book are referred to as *he* or *she* in alternating chapters,
unless their gender is apparent from the activity discusssed.

Additional photographs courtesy of: p.54 (top) © Dusty L. Perin; p55 (left)
© Reneé Stockdale.

Library of Congress Cataloging-in-Publication Data

Siino, Betsy Sikora.
    Thoroughbred spirit / words by Betsy Sikora Siino ; images by Bob
  Langrish.
      p.   cm. — (Spirit of the horse series)
    ISBN 1-889540-23-4
    1. Thoroughbred horse.   I. Title.   II. Series.
  SF293.T5S54   1998
  636.1'32—dc21   97-32163
                                                                        CIP

BowTie™ Press
3 Burroughs
Irvine, California 92618

Manufactured in the United States of America

First Printing May 1998

10 9 8 7 6 5 4 3 2 1

Table of Contents

C H A P T E R 1

The Blood Horse 5

C H A P T E R 2

The Sport of Kings 19

C H A P T E R 3

Vision of Beauty 29

C H A P T E R 4

The Next Generation 41

C H A P T E R 5

To Ride a Thoroughbred 51

E P I L O G U E

There Will Always Be an England 59

Glossary 64

The Blood Horse

The late great British Prime Minister Winston Churchill once said that there is something about the outside of a horse that is good for the inside of a man.

Spawned as he was from the rich equine culture that is England, Sir Winston knew well of what he spoke. He understood innately the drive that has for centuries spurred on humankind, notably those individuals of British extraction, to sculpt the horse like a fine slab of marble, to mold her and craft her into not only a breathtaking object of beauty, but a powerful machine of muscle and drama as well. His statement thus illuminates that indefinable swell of emotion that rises the moment one catches sight of a horse running, feet flying above the ground, shoulder muscles rippling, nostrils flaring. His

words, so characteristically succinct, capture that moment, that thrill—and so do they capture the essence of Sir Winston's fellow English native, the United Kingdom's most precious work of art, the Thoroughbred.

Though the Thoroughbred is an amalgamation of breeds who is now bred in her pure form with great care and precision all over the world, few dare to question her identity as the quintessential English horse. To understand the phenomenon that is the Thoroughbred, one must journey back three and four centuries to an age when England was an international center of commerce, politics, literature, and art—and home to a vast navy that ensured the sun would never set on its empire. England was home, too, to some of the finest horses the world had to offer.

As dominant as their island nation was as a world power throughout history, English royalty, aristocrats, and military leaders were privileged to have ample contact with such exotic horses as Arabians from the Middle East, Turkmenians from Asia, and Andalusians from Spain. Though they prized their own homegrown animals who had been sculpted so naturally by rocky, often cliff-laden terrain; sparse vegetation; and inhospitable climates, generations of savvy British horse breeders understood that other nations, too, had reason to boast of their own equine treasures. Combine the best of all, they imagined, and the result could be shattering.

This notion of cultural equine diversity would indeed prove prophetic. The process of

Chapter One

setting that concept into motion would find its roots not only within the profound English love of horses, but also within the English love of horse racing, a trait that spans back two thousand years to the time of the Roman occupation of then-named Britannia, and probably before.

Early races were run by native horses, most notably Galloway ponies, and by sporadically imported horses of Spanish and Oriental (Barb, Arabian, and Turk) extraction and mixes thereof. Through time, the sport attracted a great following among those of elite and royal position. King Henry VIII, for one, became the first royal patron of what logically became known as the Sport of Kings when he established the Royal Stud at Hampton Court during the sixteenth century.

But it was the seventeenth century and the reign of Charles II that marked the true beginnings of the Thoroughbred horse. It is this monarch who is credited with institutionalizing the practice of combining bloodlines in an attempt to create and produce the finest—and fastest—racehorse in the world. Though such hotblooded horses as Barbs, Turks, and Arabians had long made their presence known in England, under Charles' reign these animals were enlisted officially—hundreds of them, in fact—into a homegrown British breeding program that indeed resulted in the fastest horse the world has ever known.

The magical mix of an essentially unknown combination of Spanish, Oriental, and native (primarily Galloway, Welsh, and Connemara) bloodlines were responsible for the creation of the horse who became known officially as the Thoroughbred in the early nineteenth century. Yet three foreign-foaled Oriental stallions who never themselves raced are credited as the breed's foundation sires.

The first of these, the Byerley Turk, arrived on British soil in 1691 with his patron Colonel Byerley. Together the two had served valiantly in the Battle of Boyne, the light bay stallion of probable Akhal-Teke or similarly illustrious Turkmenian breeding was rumored to have saved the Colonel's life in the field. The equine war hero was thus rewarded with a life at stud in County Durham and Yorkshire. Here he established through his great-great-grandson King Herod, foaled in 1758, one of the Thoroughbred's most influential lines.

Next came the Darley Arabian, a presumably purebred Arab who arrived in England from Syria in 1704. Installed at stud in Yorkshire, this dark bay stallion's union with a mare named Betty Leedes (one of the few mares to be offered her just recognition for her contribution to the breed) resulted in the arrival in 1715 of Flying Childers. This foal ultimately blossomed into a talented athlete who never lost a race, thus earning the title as the first great Thoroughbred racehorse. Several decades later, in 1764, the Darley Arabian's great-great-grandson Eclipse was foaled and carried on the family tradition. He proved to be not only a phenomenal, unbeaten racehorse, but also so prepotent in passing his gifts on to his progeny that approximately 80 percent of twentieth-

Chapter One

century Thoroughbreds can trace their lineage back to Eclipse.

Perhaps the most well known of the three founding sires was the Godolphin Arabian or Barb. Though this small, gangly, relatively unattractive animal has long been claimed by the Arabian breed, many respected equine historians believe that the Godolphin was actually of Barb extraction. The facts regarding his arrival in England are equally murky, though he is presumed to have landed first in France from the Middle East as a gift to the king, only to be deemed unfit for a berth at the royal stables. After this, rumor has it, he may have been forced to suffer the indignity of working as a cart horse in the streets of Paris. Regardless of the veracity of that claim, he was ultimately transported across the

Channel sometime around 1728 to the stables of the Earl of Godolphin. Here he claimed his destiny at stud, founding the Matchem line, named for the Godolphin's grandson by the same name.

Today, virtually every Thoroughbred may be traced back directly to one of these three founding fathers. Their success, and that of the breeders who devised a mix of bloodlines that has never been duplicated, is evident in the fact that beginning in the seventeenth century, racing records were broken consistently for the next two hundred years. Throughout this time, as the Thoroughbred became the dominant entity on English and Irish racetracks, and on the fledgling tracks in America as well, the very nature of racing itself experienced a change. What began as races of four

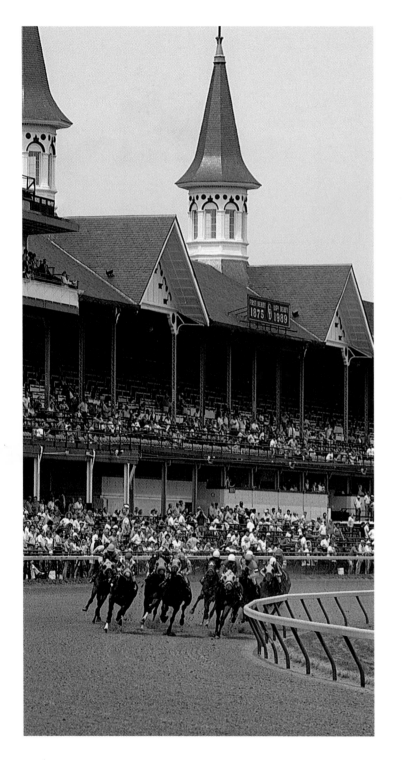

or more miles, pitting mature horses of commensurate stamina and strength against each other, would evolve into shorter contests where speed, and thus younger horses, would emerge as horseracing's heroes. Accompanying this transition was Thoroughbred racing's identity as a big business that revolves around vast, often obscene, sums of money both from the betting on and the breeding of Thoroughbred racehorses.

As this phenomenon took hold, the spiritual home of Thoroughbred racing became, and continues to be, Newmarket in Suffolk, England. Established in the seventeenth century, Newmarket has carried on the respected Thoroughbred traditions as home to several of Britain's centuries-old classic races, thousands of horses and trainers, and the Tattersalls auction house. So is it home to the British Jockey Club, which was founded in 1752 to regulate and govern the breeding of Thoroughbreds and the sport for which they are bred. Early in the Thoroughbred's conception, the United Kingdom, particularly England and Ireland, devoted itself thoroughly to the breed and its sworn vocation, which has long been practiced religiously at such racing venues as Ascot, site of some of the Royals' best-loved matches; Epson Downs, site of the classic English Derby; and Aintree, site of the Grand National Steeplechase.

America boasts its own rightful claim as second homeland to the Thoroughbred. Some of the finest British stock has made its way to the States through the years to satisfy early

and not-so-early settlers' profound passion for the Sport of Kings in a land devoid of a monarchy. So dominant did the breed become during the nineteenth century, that America's own Jockey Club was founded in 1893 and continues today as one of the nation's most prominent breed registries. While fine Thoroughbreds are bred from coast to coast, from California to Florida and everywhere in between, the heartland of America's Thoroughbred industry is Kentucky, the bluegrass state's Thoroughbred farms rivaling those of the United Kingdom in both celebrity and quality of horses produced.

Though the twentieth century has had an often devastating effect on the role of horses in society, the Thoroughbred's momentum has remained relatively untouched by contemporary history. Rooted as it is in a sport associated with the elite that attracts the attentions, and wagers, of so-called commoners as well, the Thoroughbred remains the most well-known breed of horse on the planet. Now bred passionately throughout the world, in the United Kingdom, the U.S., France, Italy, Australia, and beyond, and recruited consistently to upgrade other breeds in need of infusions of beauty and athletic ability, the Thoroughbred continues, as Winston Churchill so eloquently suggested, to warm the insides of all who behold her glory with a special brand of equine magic only the blood horse can provide.

The Sport of Kings

     Chapter Two

The year was 1973. It had been twenty-five years since a horse had won America's Triple Crown—the Kentucky Derby, the Preakness, and the Belmont. But this year at New York's Belmont Park, the anticipation was high that at last this quarter-century streak would be broken. A big red chestnut by the name of Secretariat, a son of the illustrious Bold Ruler, had won the Derby and the Preakness. Now he faced the most rigorous of the three races.

That he won was not unexpected. How he won stunned the world. Those who were fortunate to have been there still exclaim breathlessly today that it seemed they were watching a race run by a single horse, a horse who started—and finished—alone. The most

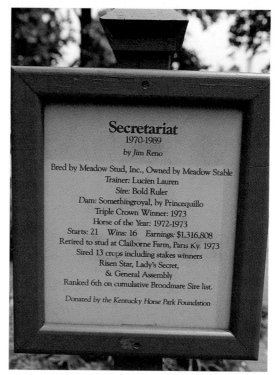

Secretariat
1970-1989
by Jim Reno

Bred by Meadow Stud, Inc., Owned by Meadow Stable
Trainer: Lucien Lauren
Sire: Bold Ruler
Dam: Somethingroyal, by Princequillo
Triple Crown Winner: 1973
Horse of the Year: 1972-1973
Starts: 21   Wins: 16   Earnings: $1,316,808
Retired to stud at Claiborne Farm, Paris Ky. 1973
Sired 13 crops including stakes winners
Risen Star, Lady's Secret,
& General Assembly
Ranked 6th on cumulative Broodmare Sire list.

Donated by the Kentucky Horse Park Foundation

vivid image emerging from the final moments of that spectacle, an image still etched into the minds of all who had witnessed the historic race either from the stands or in front of a television, is that of a lone chestnut horse with three white feet running with solitary abandon thirty-one lengths ahead of his nearest competitor. That day, Secretariat became a legend.

Of course, Secretariat is not racing's only legend. Indeed the contemporary annals of the Sport of Kings are filled with such celebrated British treasures as Hyperion, Mill Reef, and Troy, and with America's twentieth-century Triple Crown winners, including Whirlaway, Count Fleet, Citation, Seattle Slew, and Affirmed. But not since Man O' War, a phenomenal horse foaled in 1917 who won twenty of his twenty-one races, had a horse so dramatically captured the public's imagination as did Secretariat in 1973. Heralded a

wonder horse, a super horse, and the only horse ever to earn Horse of the Year honors as a two year old, when Secretariat died suddenly in 1989 the world grieved. The widespread period of mourning over a charismatic horse, whose performance will probably never be duplicated within the lifetime of his human contemporaries, validated yet again the deep human attachment mere mortals forge with those horses who seem to run faster than the speed of light.

Though the Thoroughbred has proven his mettle through the years at all manner of equine endeavor, flaunting his talents as dressage mount, show-jumping medallist, cross-country athlete, and enthusiastic hunter running to the hounds, racing, particularly flat racing, is the work for which this breed was bred and born.

For a horse lover, witnessing gleaming Thoroughbreds as they leap from the gate as a pack is more thrilling than witnessing a space launch. From zero to forty-five miles per hour in the blink of an eye, Thoroughbred racehorses leap instantly into a dead run. Their jockeys hunch over the horses' colorful silk-laden backs, exhibiting the classic seat revolutionized by turn-of-the-century American jockey James Forman "Tod" Sloan. Sloan's monkeylike position first drew disdain from colleagues and spectators in England where he raced. Yet the jeers were silenced by imitation when his fellow jockeys realized how this new position reduced stress on the backs of their young mounts and enabled a rider to whisper words of encouragement into

Chapter Two

an attentive ear, which might be all a horse needed to summon that last burst of speed in the homestretch.

Regardless of the races run, whether they be England's centuries-old classics (the One Thousand and Two Thousand Guineas, the St. Leger, the Oaks, and the illustrious English Derby); Britain's Ascot World Cup; America's big three, which are rounded out annually by the fourth American classic, the Breeder's Cup; England's Grand National Steeplechase that combines flat racing with death-defying cross-country-style jumping; or any of the countless races staged on any given day throughout the world, the heart of the show remains the Thoroughbred.

This fact is not for a moment lost on those—the royal families, old-monied aristo-crats, nouveau riche, celebrities, and digni-taries alike—who to this day continue to jostle for social position within the Sport of Kings. From the Kentucky Derby at Churchill Downs to the English Derby at Epson, the big races remain the social events of the season. These events are attended by genuine horse lovers who revel in the powerful aura of the world's fastest horses and by social climbers who strive in big hats, cutaways, and designer frocks to be seen with and, with any luck, photographed as they stand adoringly next to those animals. This is all part of a celebration of a dynasty of lovely fleet-footed horses—special spirits who are born to run. The Thoroughbred is one such spirit. In a sport designed by and for kings, this horse reigns supreme.

Vision of Beauty

When asked to describe the object of their devotion, those upon whom the Thoroughbred has cast her spell tend to speak first not of the breed's obvious beauty, but of what is referred to as heart. Though most who know the breed smile with recognition at the mention of this word, it defies a solid definition. Rather, it must be illuminated by stories of the flesh-and-blood horses themselves and the heart that has made them legendary.

Heart is that font of mystical internal energy that propels the Thoroughbred forward through all adversity. On the track, evidence of heart flies skyward in the spray of turf a horse's hooves release as the animal pummels the ground in an earnest attempt to vanquish that pesky bay approaching on the inside.

Vision of Beauty

Heart is evident when the steeplechaser, having lost her rider many lengths back, forges ahead, approaches a seemingly insurmountable combination of fences and water, and then soars like Pegasus over the hellish jumble of obstacles. Heart may be heard in the labored breathing of the seasoned, sweat-soaked filly, who forces one more gulp of oxygen into beleaguered lungs that seem close to bursting as she stretches a slender foreleg across the finish line. Heart is paramount, too, within that athlete who makes the ultimate sacrifice, the horse who upon entering the last curve of the track acknowledges the stab of pain that shoots up the lower reaches of a leg yet refuses to allow the broken bone at the root of that pain to interfere with the incorruptible quest to claim immortality.

Heart lives and breathes within the Thoroughbred, a breed customarily christened the classic horse, a horse of profound beauty who runs faster for longer distances than any other horse on the planet. Essentially four types of these horses, each equal in heart, are found on racetracks today.

The most well known of the flat-racing Thoroughbreds is the middle-distance horse, the star of the classic races—the Derbys, the Guineas, and the like—a horse with sloped shoulders and croups that typically run as three-year-olds for distances of one-and-a-half to one-and-three-quarter miles. The sprinter is typically a taller, younger horse graced with more speed than stamina so as to conquer tracks of approximately 1100 to 1590 yards quickly. The stayer is a later-maturing,

Chapter Three

shorter-bodied horse, prized for her stamina, which keeps her going longer and faster than other horses against whom she may be pitted. And lastly, there is the steeplechaser, the Thoroughbred who is bred to jump as well as run. This horse, a particular jewel in Ireland's Thoroughbred crown, runs cross-country courses and steeplechases with strength, endurance, and powerful hindquarters that propel her up and over any and all treacherous obstacles in her path.

Though Thoroughbred conformation may vary depending on type, there is typically no mistaking this breed for any other horse. The classic Thoroughbred stands somewhere from 15 to 17 hands tall and exhibits athletic greatness in every component of her physique: sloping shoulders; prominent with-

Vision of Beauty

ers; clean joints; long, slender legs; and small hooves. So is this athlete, who is typically chestnut, bay, gray, or black in color, also quite beautiful, her athletic appearance accented by a small, elegant head with a straight profile, large eyes and nostrils, and a long graceful neck.

Given her substantial gifts, it is not surprising that the Thoroughbred is one of, if not the most influential breeds of horse in the world (a statement the Arabian would be more than willing to contest). The blood of the blood horse has been coveted by breeders all over the world who have sought to enhance their own breeds with a blast of Thoroughbred fire, a gift that blends beautifully with virtually any other equine gene pool.

Chapter Three

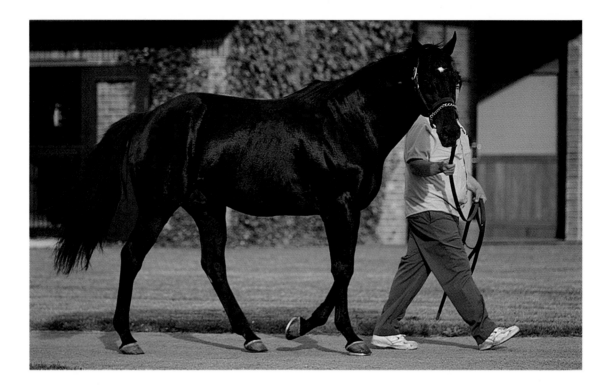

Throughout the world there exist horses of all extractions who may thank the Thoroughbred for her contributions to their genetic blueprints. One group that is infinitely beholden to the Thoroughbred is that of the European warmbloods: the Oldenburger, the Dutch Warmblood, the Hanoverian, the Trakehner, and the like. Named warmblood because they have been created through the mixing of both cold blooded (calm, cool, draft-type) horses and those of a hotter head, these large, stunning horses would not exist as they do today were it not for the prominent position of the Thoroughbred in their breeding programs. As fans of world-class equine competition are well aware, the result has been phenomenal, the warmbloods consistently taking top honors in dressage, show jumping, and three-day eventing thanks to an ample infusion of hot Thoroughbred blood. This sweet nectar has not only refined them physically, but fortified them with an unbeatable athletic prowess borne of the commingling of hot and cold.

 Chapter Three

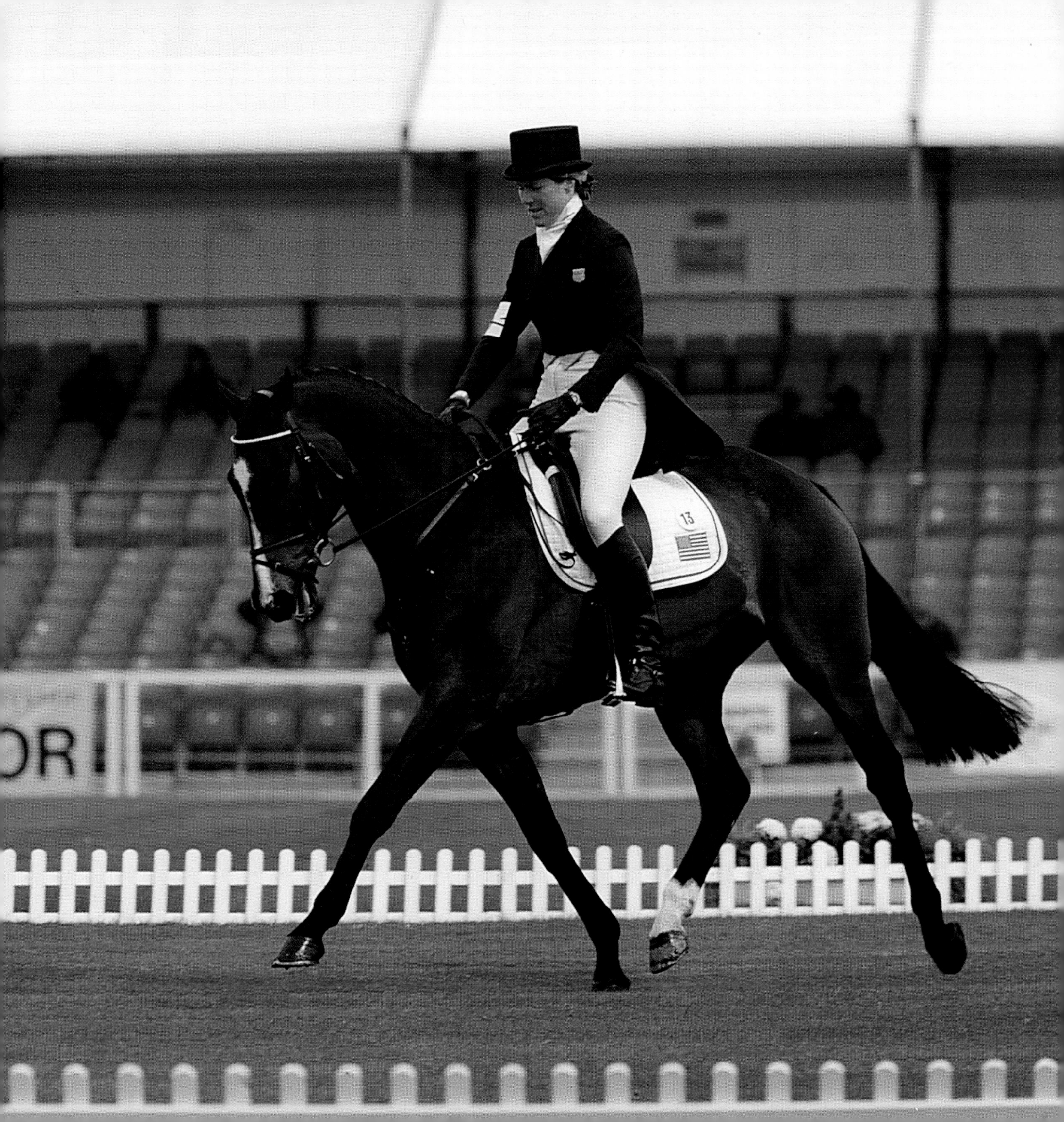
OR
13

The Next Generation

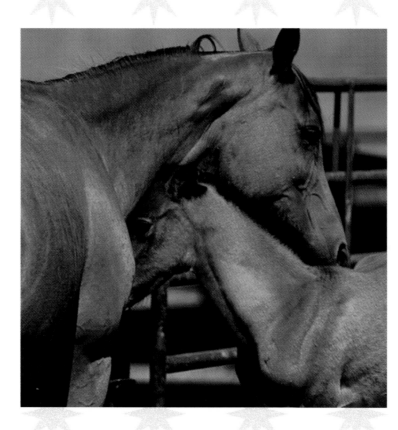

New Year's Day is a momentous occasion throughout the world, but within the Thoroughbred world, it is cause for a special celebration. January 1st is the Thoroughbred's birthday—every Thoroughbred's birthday. On that day, every Thoroughbred is proclaimed one year older.

But of course most Thoroughbreds are not foaled on New Year's Day—in fact spring is traditionally the season when the broodmare's eleven-month gestation reaches its climax. Much preparation is invested in that moment: months of pedigree evaluations and negotiations, prenatal veterinary care and conditioning, and dreams of the expected foal's promise.

When that day arrives—for example a soft, warm day in April—the excitement is almost

The Next Generation

43

palpable in the air of the foaling barn at a topflight Kentucky Thoroughbred farm. A seasoned broodmare with great rounded sides stands quietly in the straw. This is all routine for her. She has produced many a fleet-footed foal and will soon welcome a new addition to her clan. Her mate this time around ran the Derby. His granddad raced at Epson and Ascot and carried the blood of Eclipse in his veins. What story will the newborn be destined to write?

That story begins now. The mare delivers her precious bundle with ease. A colt. A chestnut with three white feet. Just like Secretariat. Could it be a sign of greatness to come? Such superstitions run deep in the racing world.

Chapter Four

The new arrival, still damp from the birthing process, wriggles a moment in the clean straw. He then peers around with a somewhat startled gaze at Mom, who seems somehow familiar. Somewhat flustered, even frightened, by the stares and whispers from the two-legged creatures standing by, his attentions turn to the challenge before him, a challenge leveled by the internal voice that speaks to all prey animals, even those within such protected environments. Though he is newly arrived, he knows it is time to stand. Though there are no predators about, he knows he must obey that voice. Now he must convince his legs to comply. One day he will rely on these legs, now so long and spindly, so difficult to coordinate into one cohesive motion, to carry him with grace and speed

over the turf. But now he simply wishes to move them beneath his body and test their ability to bear weight.

It's a struggle, but at last he succeeds. He wobbles over to Mom. She nuzzles him and looks around with a calm eye at those she trusts within the stall. They praise her for another job well done. The youngster seeks instinctively the source of nourishment at Mom's belly. His mother stands calmly, serenely, and closes her eyes.

The next day marks the foal's first introduction to the legendary bluegrass of Kentucky. He follows his mother out to the pasture. The pungent spring air fills his nostrils, the aroma triggering an unexplained sense of recognition. His interest fully captured now, he spies another youngster over by

the fence. And another by a large old oak tree. The other foals return his gaze, and though equally curious they are content, like him, to remain safely by their mothers' sides.

In the days to come, however, a new sense of courage takes hold of the young foal. He begins to venture farther and farther away from his dam, all the while mastering the mechanics of those long legs of his that so efficiently transport him from one end of the pasture to the other. Then one day, an uncontrolled momentum overtakes him, the inner fire that is the thread that binds all Thoroughbreds, both past and present, together as one. He runs. His other young pasturemates heed his example and approach from behind. They are welcome to join him in his joyous sprint, but by instinct the front-

runner increases his speed to protect his lead from their grasp. Leaning on the white fence rails, two men and a woman watch the youngsters whose legs blur as they discover their wings. The spectators smile. This is what they had hoped for: Thoroughbred heart in the making.

The young foal must become accustomed to such attentions. In time, the three at the fence will become thousands in the stands. So must he adjust to the daily routine of stable life. He is taught almost immediately to wear a tiny foal halter, and though he balks at first, he eventually agrees to abide by the tug of the lead rope that guides him to the pasture in the morning. He grows accustomed to the soothing sensation of the brush over his thin, sensitive Thoroughbred skin, and to hands

stroking the soft velvet of his coat. He even learns to tolerate the handling of his feet—but only if the resident barn cat, a traditional racehorse totem, is nearby. Another milestone occurs sometime between his fourth and sixth month when he comes to prefer the rich sweet grass of the pasture to his mother's milk, a transition made easier in the company of other foals faced with the same maternal separation.

From learning to walk calmly alongside a lead horse to the racetrack gate, to the sensation of the first weight of a saddle—and then a rider—on his back, new experiences will come early to the youngster. He will learn fast. He must. Thoroughbreds grow up quickly. Eight months from the foal's arrival, on New Year's Day, the farm celebrates a

birthday: the collective birthday of the foals, all one year old today—in Thoroughbred years, that is. Within the next two short years, perhaps one among them will emerge the next Man O' War. The next Affirmed. The next Secretariat. Perhaps not. But it never hurts to dream. In the midst of those dreams, the Thoroughbreds, young and mature alike, will continue to run. They will run not because they know it is expected of them, but because they have no choice. They must run just as they must breathe. It's in the blood.

The Next Generation

CHAPTER FIVE

To Ride a Thoroughbred

To pigeonhole the Thoroughbred into a single role, to assume that he is a racehorse and nothing but a racehorse, is to risk the wrath of the minions who have known and worked with this breed in a variety of capacities for hundreds of years. Though the Thoroughbred was indeed bred originally for the track, English and Irish horsepeople in the early days of the breed's development recognized quickly that the Thoroughbred could jump just as exquisitely as he could run. We are thus today blessed with a fine family of Thoroughbred athletes who excel on local, regional, national, and world-class levels at all the English disciplines: dressage, hunters, jumpers, and three-day eventing.

To Ride a Thoroughbred

53

While this all-around athlete may be a horse who all people can appreciate, he is not an appropriate mount for the masses. Though the healthy population of the contemporary Thoroughbred has now made the breed affordable to those not necessarily of the manor-born, what people of all economic levels must possess for a successful partnership with this hotblooded, high-powered animal is serious equestrian training. In this respect, the Thoroughbred is a horse to whom fledgling equestrians may aspire, an equine muse inspiring those struggling to master the elements of classical horsemanship. The reward to those who pursue this goal with a purity of heart and determination is the ultimate gift: To ride a Thoroughbred.

Those who reach that apex may compete on behalf of their horses for high honors that recognize the breed's equine talents beyond the track. Through cooperative efforts between such organizations as the Performance Horse Registry (PHR, an affiliate of The Jockey Club that recognizes Thoroughbred excellence in non-racing disciplines), Thoroughbred Horses for Sport, the United States Dressage Federation (USDF), and the United States Combined Training Association (USCTA), Thoroughbreds at all levels of competition may receive their just rewards. The mission of this respected network is to ensure that the world never for a moment underestimates the magnitude of this spectacular athlete's talents.

While there exists no Thoroughbred breed show per se, virtually any all-breed horse show is a Thoroughbred show, whether that be the Olympics, Devon, or a schooling show at the local barn. Regardless of the venue, the Thoroughbreds in attendance invariably wow the judges and the crowds with their beauty and power, as well as a grace and dignity that somehow seem to defy their breed's fiery image.

In California, we might find a big bay Thoroughbred performing the intricate balletic moves of classical horsemanship that lie at the heart of dressage. The young woman on his back signals to him with unseen pressure of her legs in a communion borne of the hours of practice the two have spent together in the schooling ring. The big bay follows the predetermined pattern marked within the arena with an almost clairvoyant understanding of what is expected of him. Strong repeat performances in similar events sanctioned by the United States Dressage Federation, and the commensurate points they garner, could earn this horse a coveted Silver Stirrup Award

To Ride a Thoroughbred

from the PHR in conjunction with the USDF All Breeds Awards Program.

In Michigan, we find a gray hunter flying over jumps in a large show arena, evoking the image of former American Olympic Thoroughbred Gem Twist. He, too, could qualify for Silver Stirrup honors, even though his pedigree indicates he is but half Thoroughbred. The powers that be of the PHR acknowledge what breeders worldwide have known for centuries: that nothing blends better than Thoroughbred blood. A horse of pure Thoroughbred breeding can be a bit hot for some riders in some disciplines, yet temper this with the influence of a cooler breed, say, quarter horse or Welsh cob, and together each can impart individual gifts to their progeny, producing a calmer

horse, such as our gray here, blessed with dynamic Thoroughbred skills.

Meanwhile in Virginia, a chestnut mare is tackling a cross-country course as part of a three-day event sanctioned by the USCTA. Rounding out her performance are a day of dressage and a day of show jumping, the results validating her eligibility for awards not only from the USCTA and the PHR, but also from Thoroughbred Horses for Sport, which celebrates Thoroughbreds with its own awards program for a variety of disciplines at schooling and rated shows nationwide.

That the Thoroughbred is a quintessential athlete skilled at running, jumping, and dressage is no secret, of course, but now the word is spreading that those who compete in these disciplines at all levels, even

local and regional levels, can reap the same Thoroughbred glory as their racing brethren. The good news is that a horse need not boast a million-dollar price tag or a record-setting race record, and his rider need not be born a Royal to qualify.

There Will Always Be an England

For centuries humankind has dreamt of flying horses. The winged creatures populate our REM-induced imaginings and carry us up above the clouds, floating with an organic grace and muscle that could never be duplicated by a plane, helicopter, or hot-air balloon. But are these animals truly just figments of our imaginations? It appears not. Indeed a flying horse lives among us today. That horse, the Thoroughbred, may not take wing in the classic sense, but when she runs, some swear she truly seems to sprout wings and soar.

Well seasoned in her role as spiritual guide, the Thoroughbred is often the conduit by which most individuals, particularly impressionable young girls, are ushered into the illustrious world of horses. One accidental glimpse of a gleaming chestnut streaking like a bolt of lightning across a television screen, and the die is cast. In that single moment of time, the horse, a creature who at first impression seems a ghostly enigma, is transformed into a magical being. Yet that mythical equine ambassador is a flesh-and-blood animal who lives and breathes today just as she did more than two hundred years ago on the tracks and breeding farms of Newmarket, England. That was obviously the plan at the moment of her conception. The breeders responsible for nurturing the tender seed that would blossom into the Thoroughbred must surely have known that they were creating a treasure for all time. Such miracles do not occur by chance.

There Will Always Be an England

Wherever and whenever there is the ancient calling to breed fast horses—and the money to finance that dream—there will be Thoroughbreds. This animal, one of the most influential horses on the planet, is the United Kingdom's greatest, most lasting legacy to the world. In paying tribute to the Thoroughbred, one must thus equally honor her native home, for without one there is no other.

In the spirit of the grandeur of this collective legacy, there lies the often unacknowledged fact that this horse is more than merely a speed machine. An inner magic within her soul, the legendary heart that regardless of circumstance dulls the horse's pain and propels her forward in the infinite quest to fulfill her genetic callings, has inspired humans for centuries to both breed and immortalize this

horse. Though the breed is a profoundly beautiful member of the equine family, inspiration for countless works of art in oils, bronze, and marble, it is the Thoroughbred heart that has long enchanted artists so. That heart found its roots in the early stud farms, hunt courses, and racetracks of the United Kingdom. We thus owe the creators at the core of the early Thoroughbred breeding efforts, all of them artists in their own right, a debt of gratitude.

The cold, gray, and dismal world that would exist without the Thoroughbred is unthinkable. Trusting the potential immortal significance of their mission, those early breeders worked toward a seemingly unattainable goal to produce a horse of beauty, speed, stamina, and heart who would part the overcast skies of England and sweep out like a whirlwind into the world at large. Though the breathtaking, hotblooded product of their machinations has changed little over time, the world into which she was thrust more than two centuries ago has changed dramatically. Today, the sun now sets on the British Empire. But regardless of what future events transpire on her home turf, there will always be the mythical entity that is the Thoroughbred. And as long as there is the Thoroughbred, there will always be an England.

There Will Always Be an England

Glossary

blood horse: another term for the Thoroughbred

colt: an uncastrated male horse between the ages of one and four years

croup: the top line of the hindquarters; rump

dam: the mother of a horse

dressage: a form of exhibition riding in which the horse receives nearly invisible cues from the rider and performs a series of difficult steps and gaits with lightness of step and perfect balance. Dressage also is a classical training method that teaches the horse to be responsive, attentive, willing, and relaxed for the purpose of becoming a better equine athlete.

flat race: a race on a course with no obstacles to jump

foal: a horse of either sex aged one year or under

halter: a headpiece of leather, rope, or nylon used to lead a horse

hand: a standard of equine height measurement derived from the width of a human hand. Each hand equals 4 inches, with fractions expressed in inches. A horse who is 16.2 hands is 16 hands, 2 inches, or 66 inches tall at the withers.

heart: a quality in a horse that demonstrates a desire to perform as well as possible in response to a demand

hotblood: a high-spirited and active horse descended from Mid-Eastern or North African ancestors

hunter: a horse bred and trained to be ridden for the sport of hunting; a show hunter is a horse who is bred to be well mannered and elegant over fences in English classes

pedigree: the recorded list of a horse's ancestors

steeplechase: a cross-country horse race that is run over a specially prepared obstacle course

three-day event: a competition involving dressage, cross-country, and show jumping that tests the versatility and ability of both horse and rider, and continues over three consecutive days

warmblood: a term used to describe distinct breeds usually named according to the region in which the breed was developed. These large, well-muscled horses possess the calm temperament of their cold-blood draft ancestors and the athleticism of their hotblood forebears, making them suitable for dressage and show jumping.

withers: the highest part of a horse's back, where the neck and the back join